HARLAN COUNTY PROUD | 3

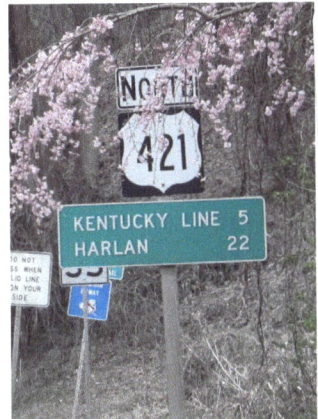

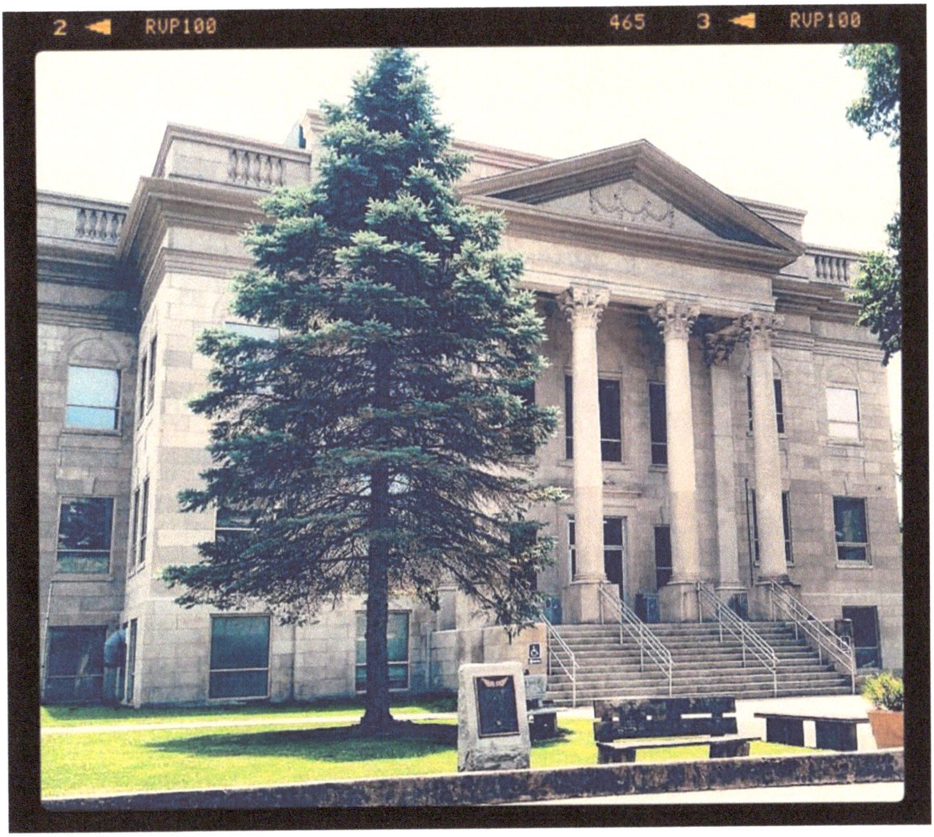

We all know the story of how the Harlan County courthouse was burned by confederates during the civil war. But did you know this is actually the fifth courthouse of Harlan County and the second to sit on this site.? The present Harlan County courthouse was constructed in 1918-22. The courthouse is built using Indiana limestone and is a two-story, stone structure with a Beaux-Arts influence.

The initial site for the first three courthouses in Harlan located on a mound in the city, which due to this mound was initially called Mount Pleasant. Turns out that this was an Indian burial mound, as further digging an excavation during the building of subsequent buildings onsite revealed bones and other artifacts. When the courthouse was moved to the present site pictured above, the old courthouse remained, and was later used as a meeting hall and Masonic lodge.

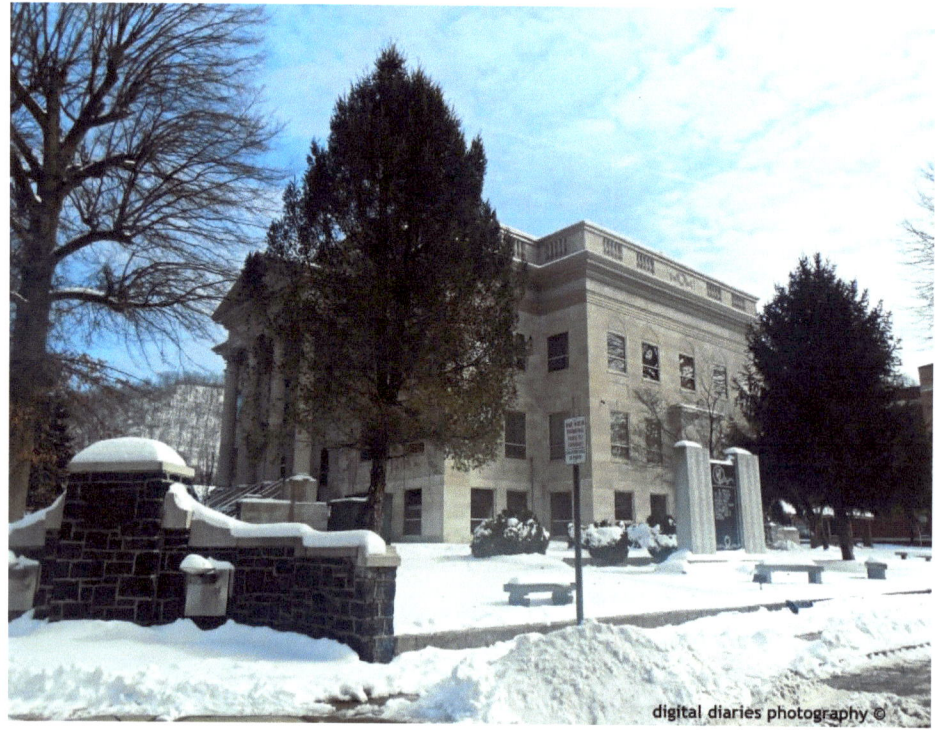

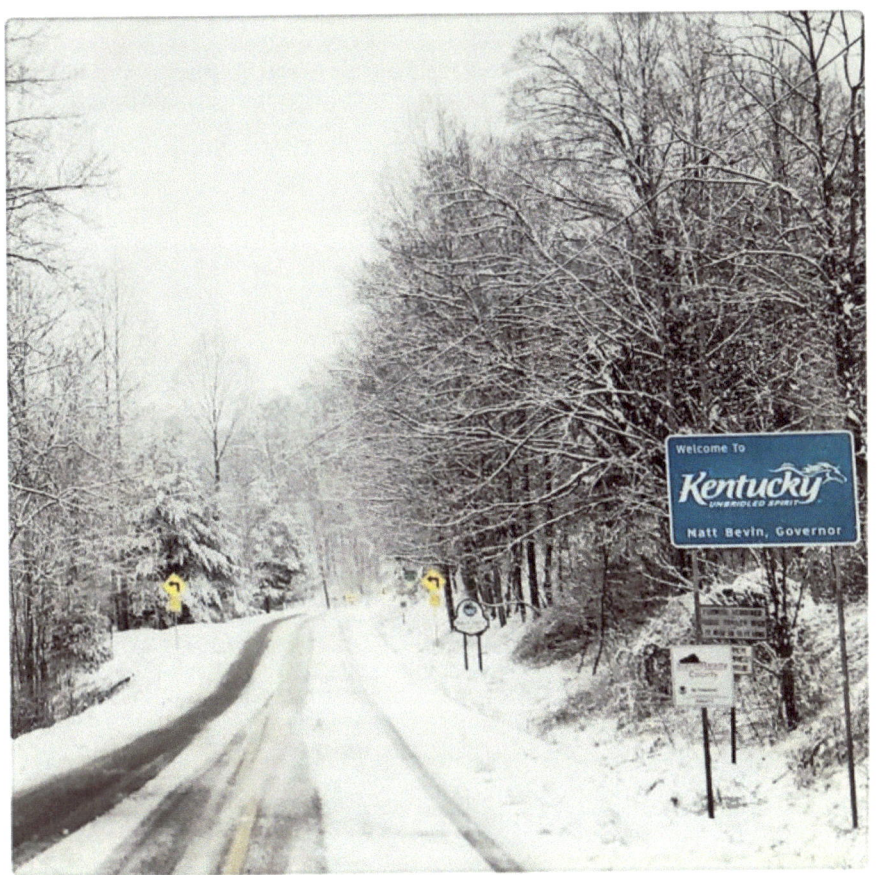

Welcome to Harlan County

Preface

Harlan County is a very diverse and varied county. From the preserved coal mining towns of the tri cities area to the recreation area heavy areas such as Martin's Fork Lake and the Black Mountain Off Road Park to the rugged beauty that is Little Shepherd Trail. Highlighted in this book are some of my favorite places in this wonderful county that I am proud to call home. Some of these are well known landmarks, others are off the beaten path and even a couple that I just recently discovered myself.

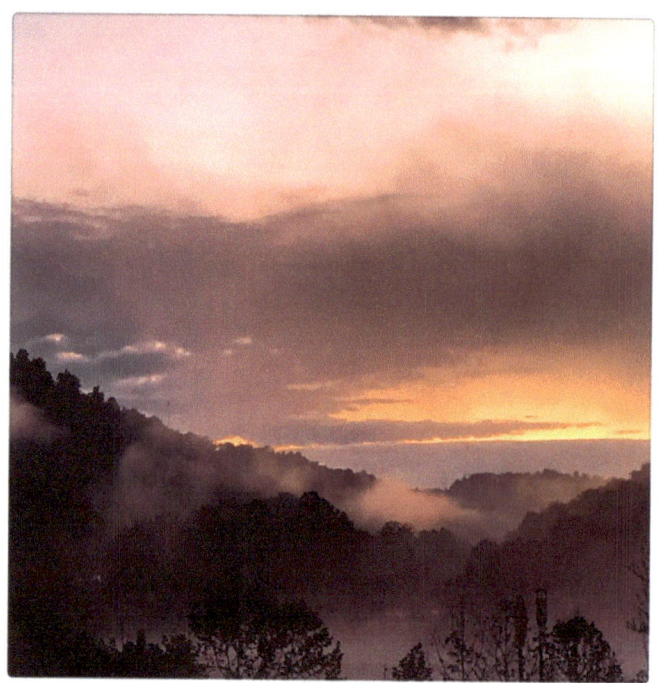

A Quick History of Harlan County

In 1780 the Virginia legislature divided Kentucky County, which included all of present day Kentucky into three counties, Fayette, Jefferson and Lincoln. In 1792 the three new counties were incorporated to the new nation as the state of Kentucky. In 1799, part of Lincoln County, including the area which is present day Harlan County was separated to form Knox County.

In 1819 Harlan County was formed from part of Knox County. Named for A pioneer and Major in the Continental Army, Silas Harlan, the county was the 60th Kentucky County formed. In 1842 the county's area was reduced when Letcher County was formed from parts of Harlan and Perry County. The area was reduced further in 1867 when Bell County was formed from parts of Harlan and Bell Counties; and again in 1878 when Leslie County was formed.

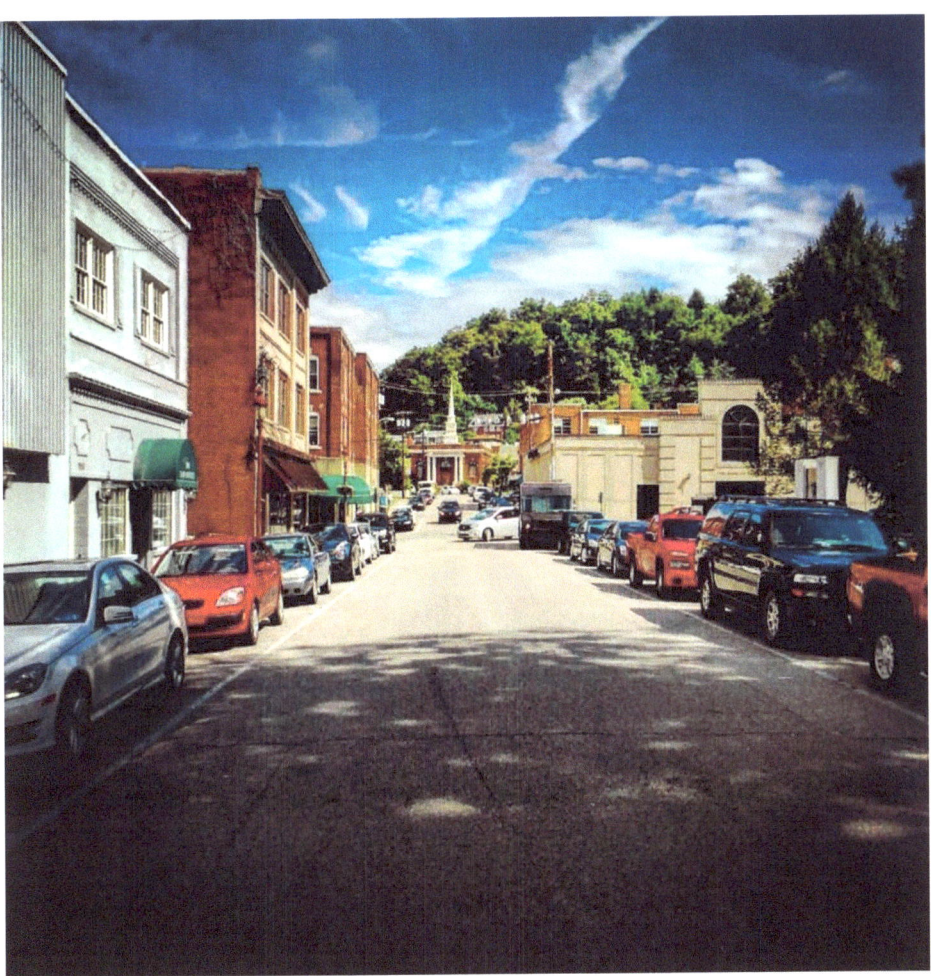

First Street, Downtown Harlan

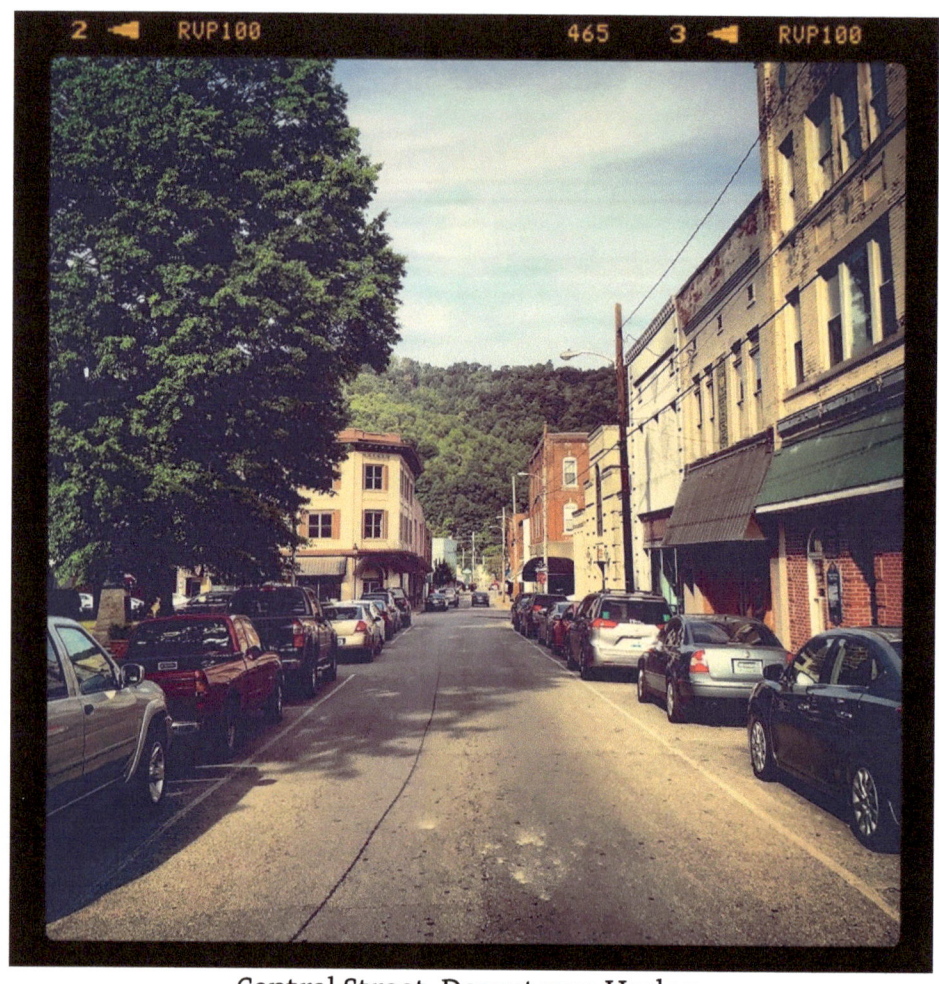
Central Street, Downtown Harlan

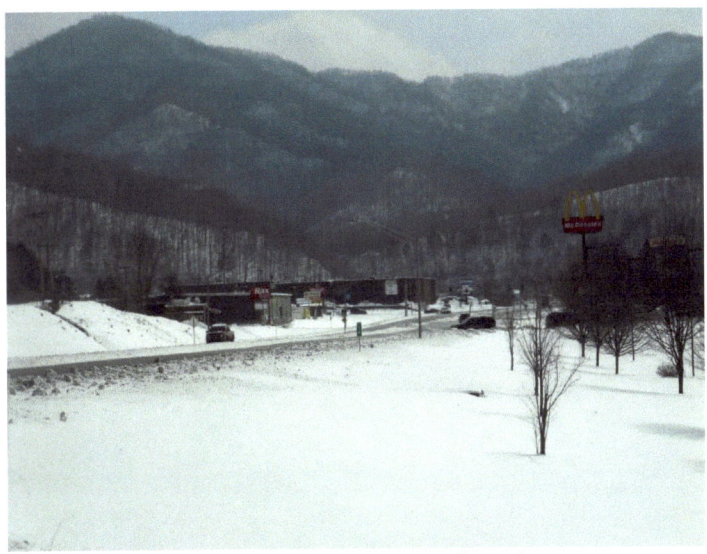

US 421 Bypass at Browning Acres

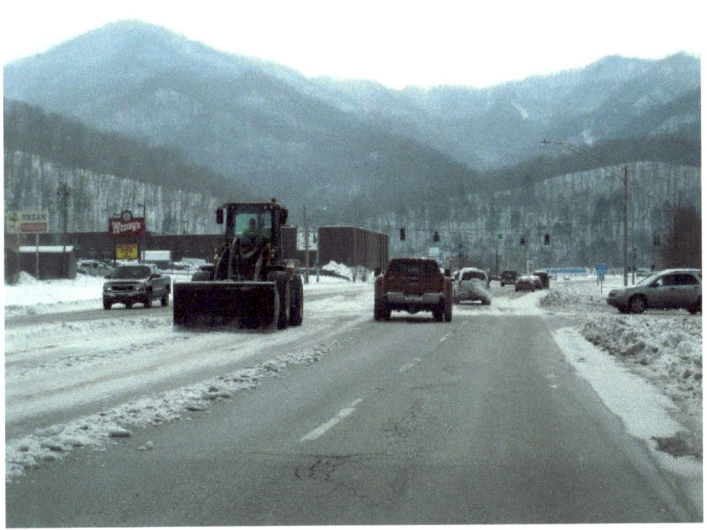

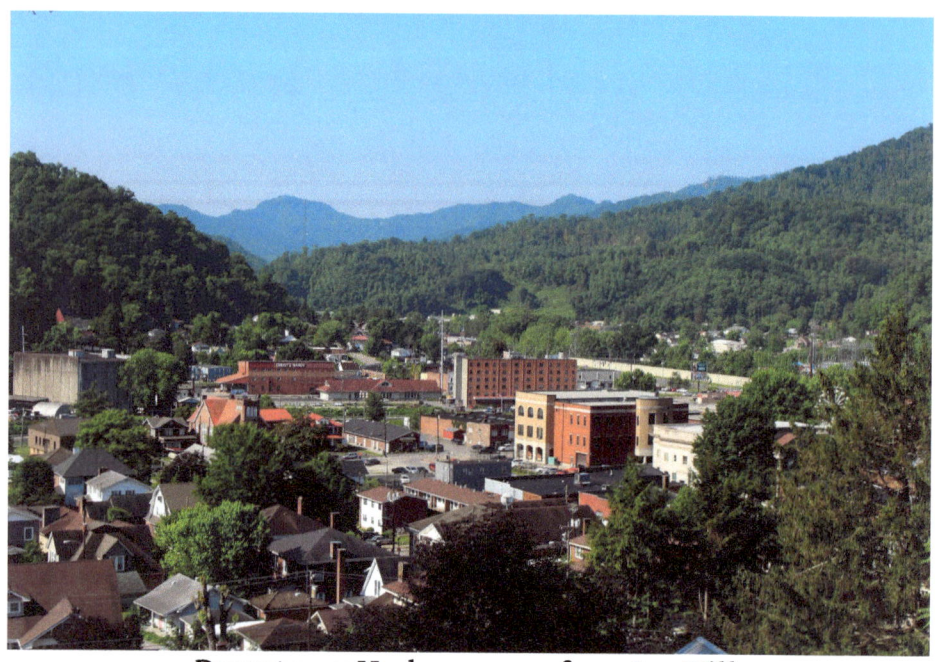

Downtown Harlan as seen from Ivy Hill

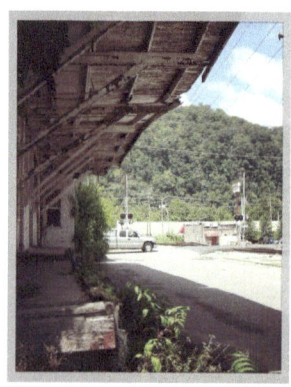

Jellico Grocery / Hackney Building Railroad Street

Harlan (now demolished)

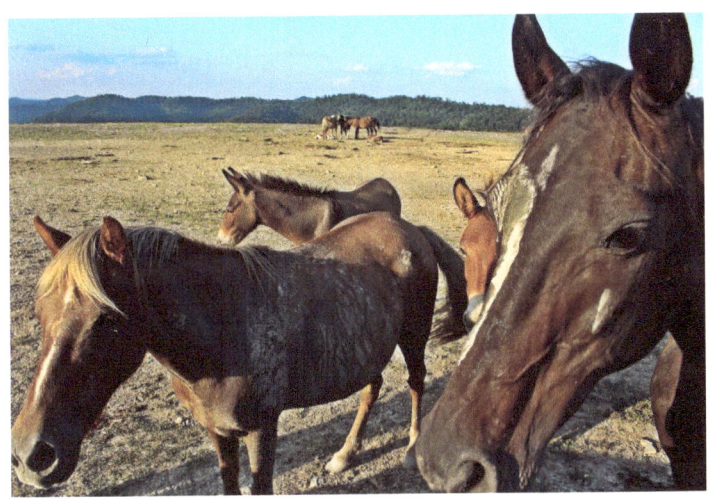

There are well over one hundred wild horses that roam this abandoned stirp mine property in Harlan County near the Leslie County line.

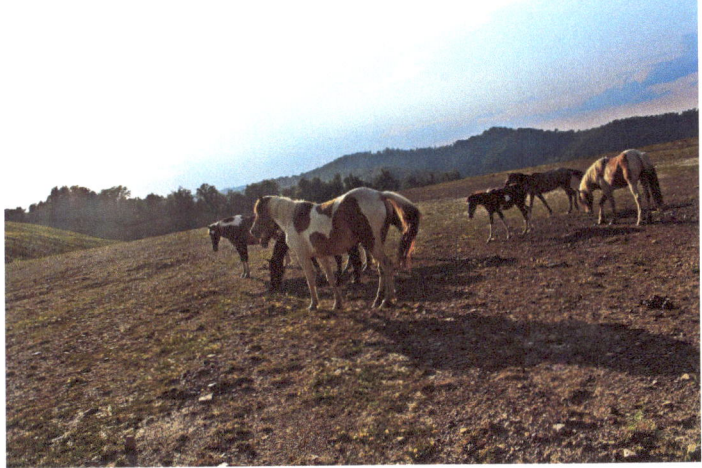

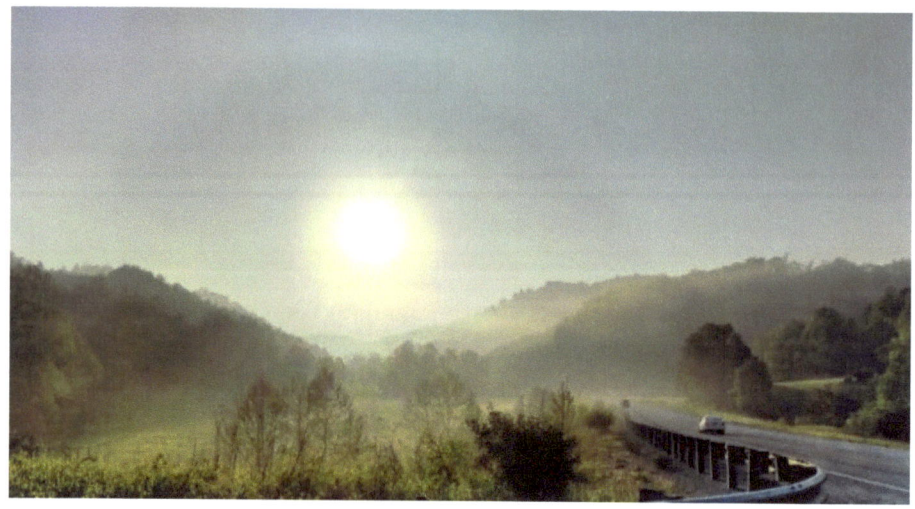

US 119 Near Cumberland

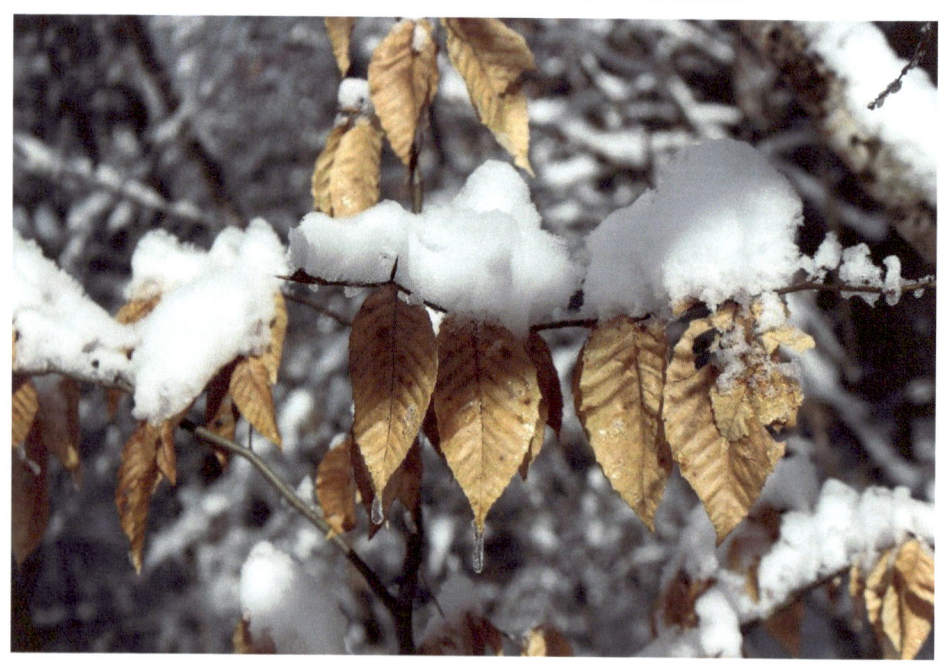

The Coal Miner's Memorial Theater in Benham.

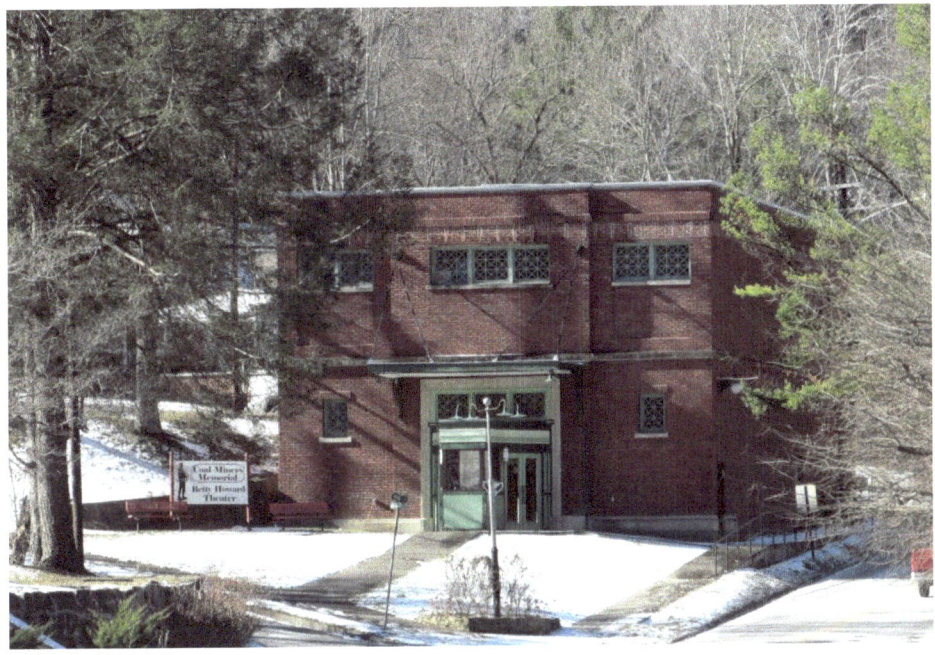

The Theater was built in 1922. The Benham Theater closed in the late 1950s and was later donated to the city of Benham to be used as a Youth Center. The building, along with several others in Benham were placed on the National Register of Historic Places in 1984. Today the theater has been fully restored and is used by the city for community functions.

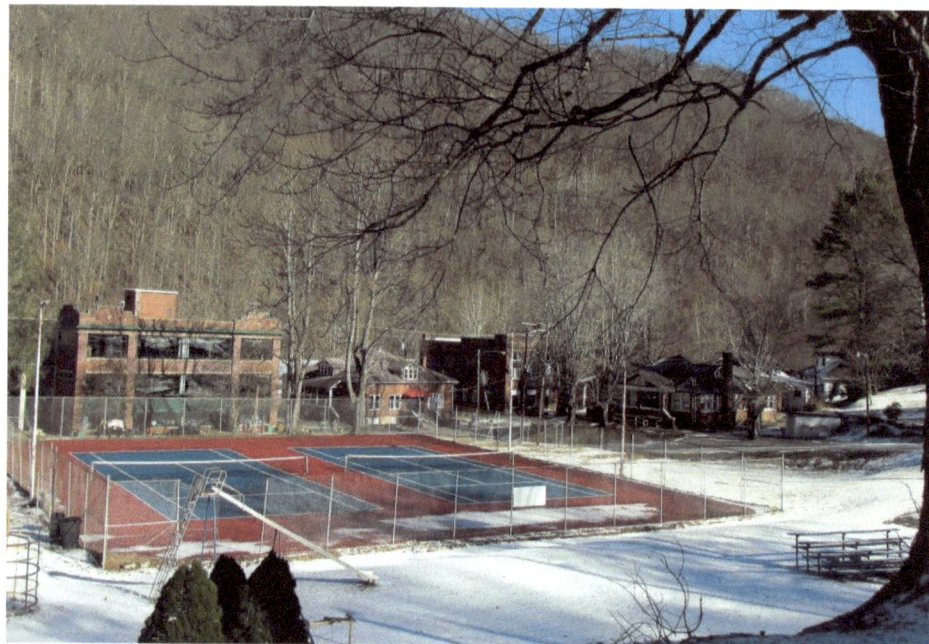

Benham was founded in 1909 by Wisconsin Steel Corporation/ International Harvester Company. At its peak operation, there were 1200 employees and their families residing in Benham. Today tourists can visit the Kentucky Coal Mining Musuem located in the former Company store and spend the night and enjoy some delicious food at the Benham School House Inn that is housed in the former Benham High School

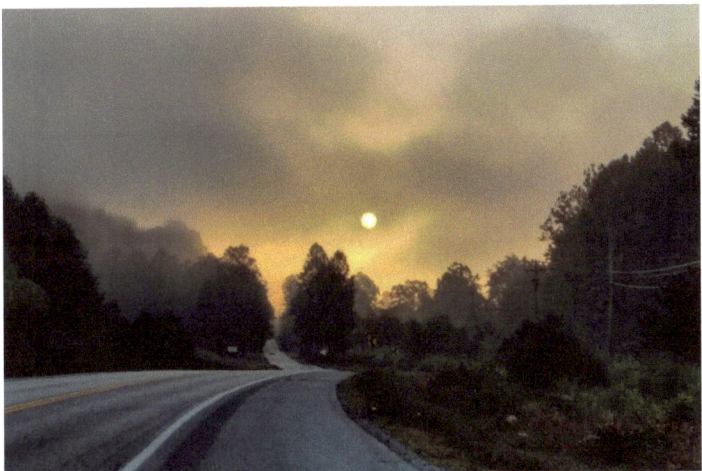

Early morning on US 421 South of Harlan

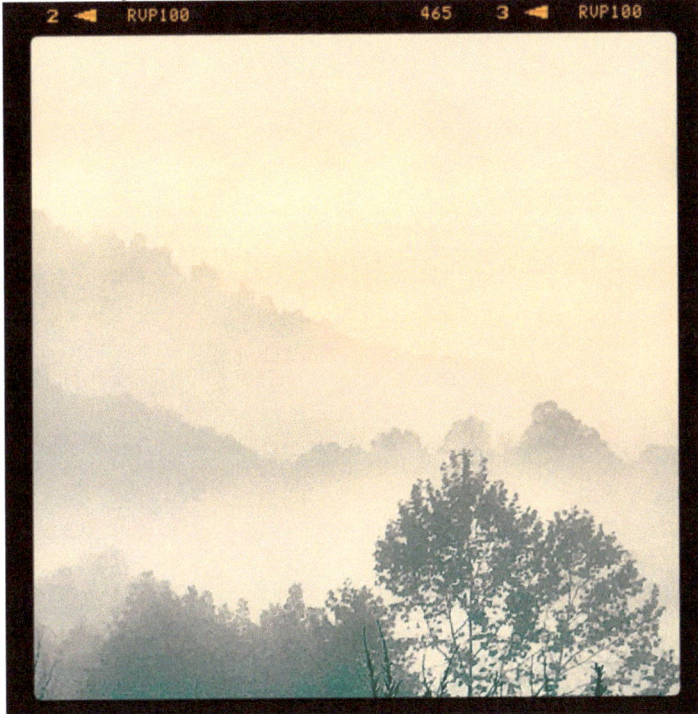

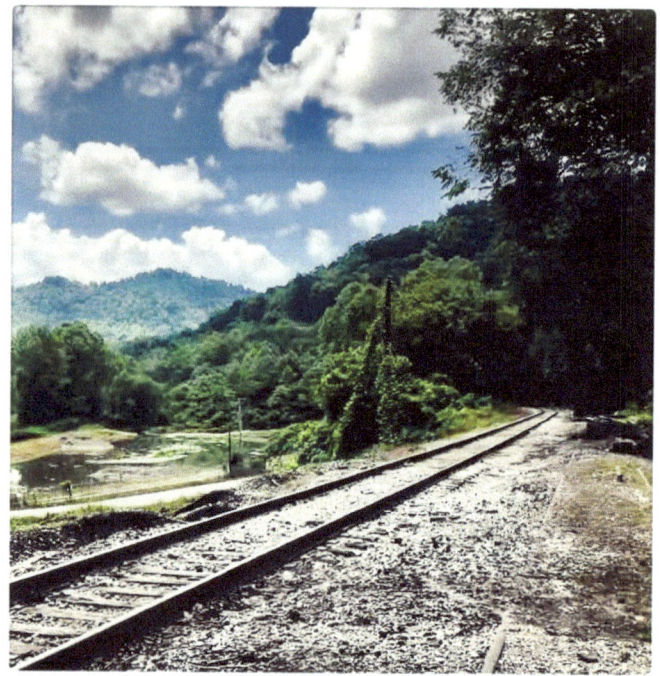

Mary Helen

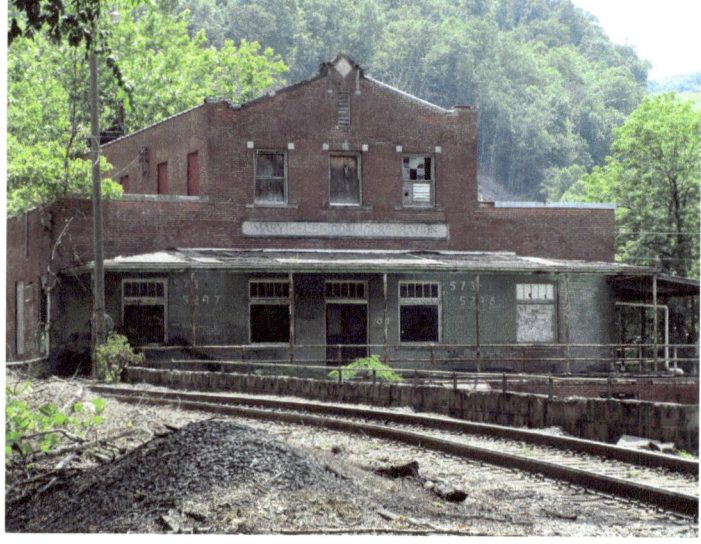

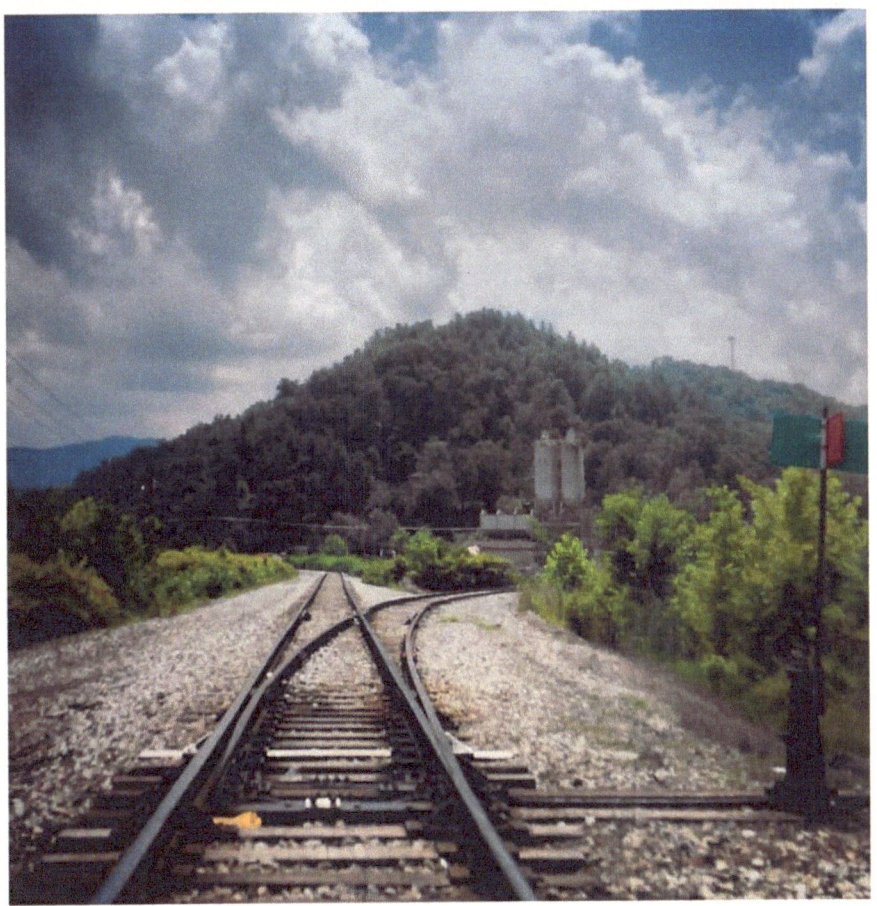

Dressen

Lynch

Founded in 1917 by the U.S. Coal and Coke Company, Lynch grew to be the largest company town in Kentucky and arguably the country with a population of over 10,000 people. The town was named for "the father of mine safety", Thomas Lynch. During the 1960s modernization lead to declines in the coal industry and US Coal and Coke tore down much of the town and sold what was left to the inhabitants.

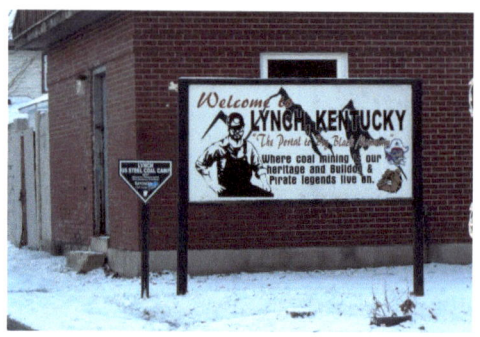

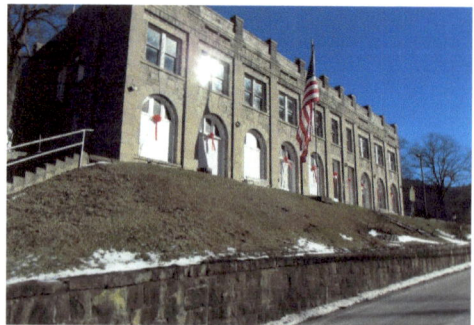

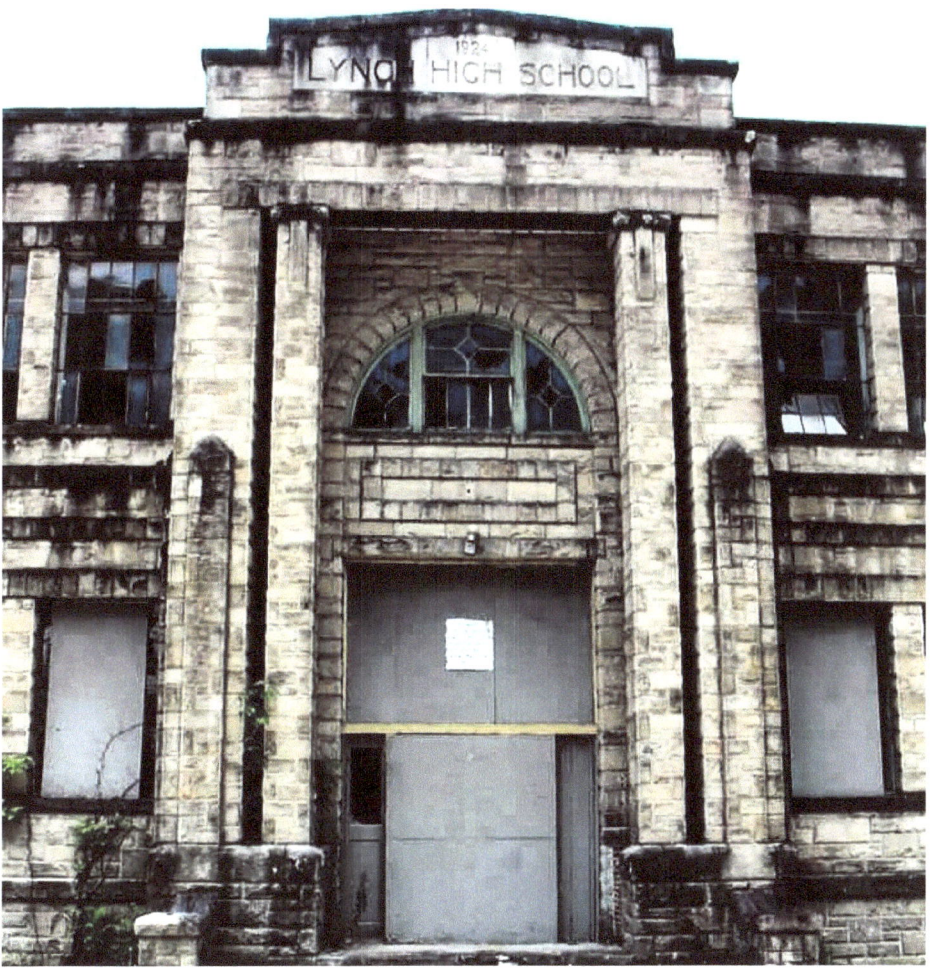

Lynch High School opened its doors in 1924. The entire town of Lynch, including the public schools were paid for and ran by the US Coal and Coke Company which is a subsidiary of US Steel. The schools, along with many of the other company constructed buildings in town were built of cut sand stone. Many people believe that US Steel thought they would be in Lynch mining coal for more than a century.

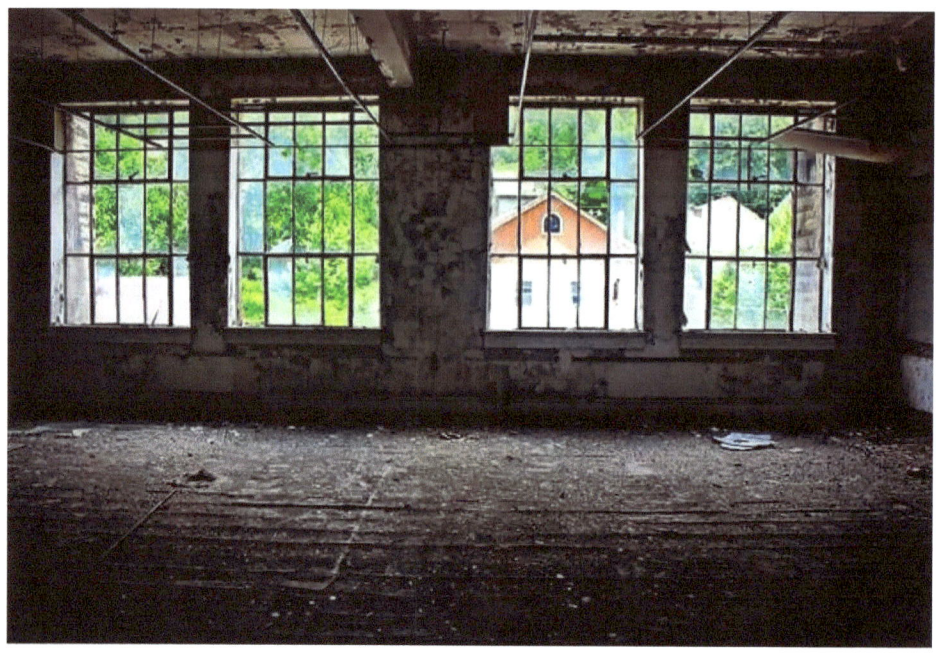

In 1981 the Lynch School District merged with the Harlan County School District and Lynch High School closed. Students from Lynch were sent to Cumberland High School.

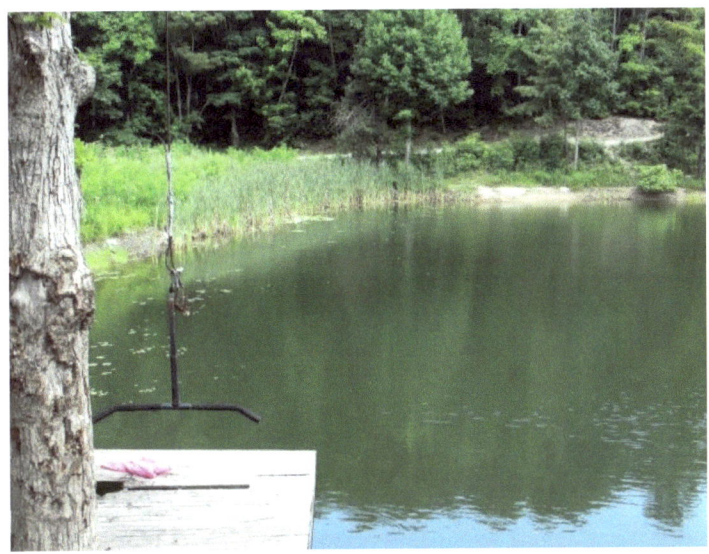

One of Harlan County's best kept secrets, Cupp Lake

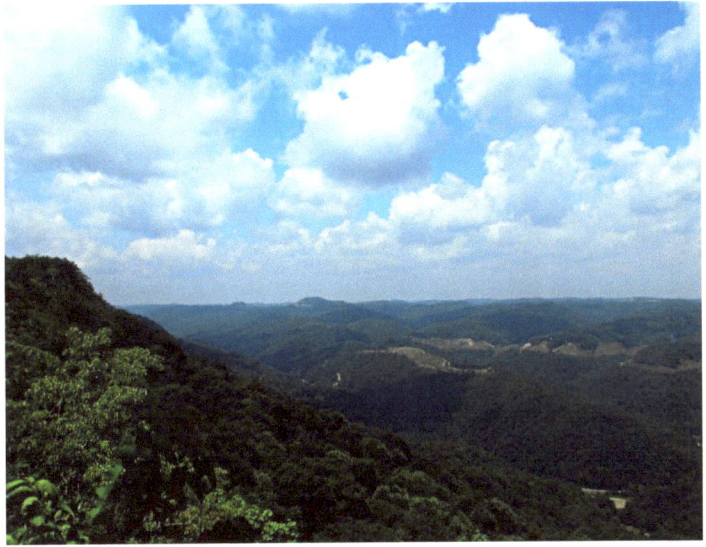

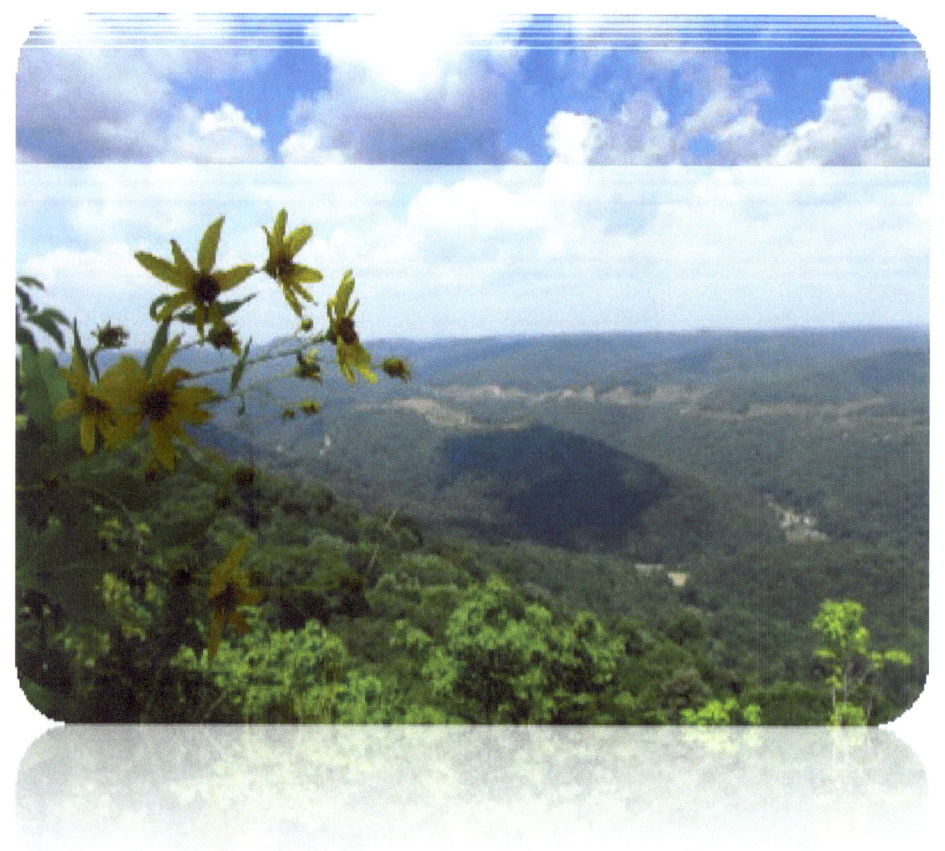

Kingdom Come State Park

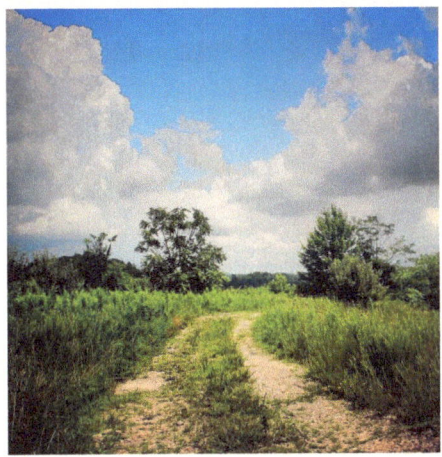

Little Shepherd Trail

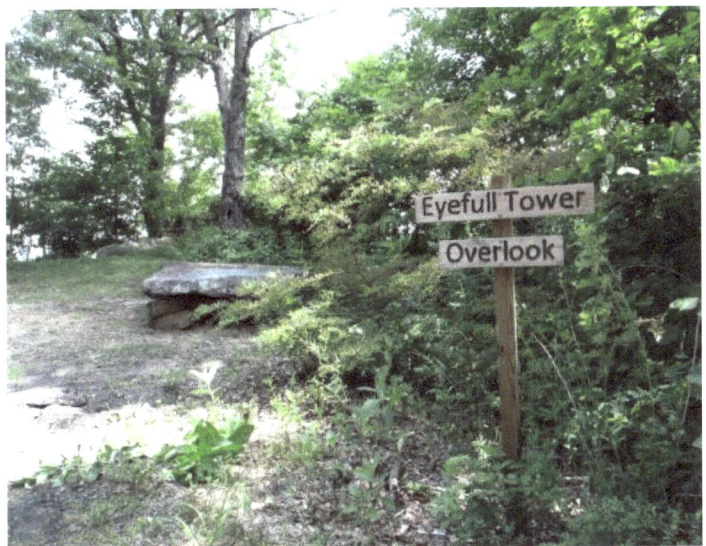

Summer Day in Harlan County

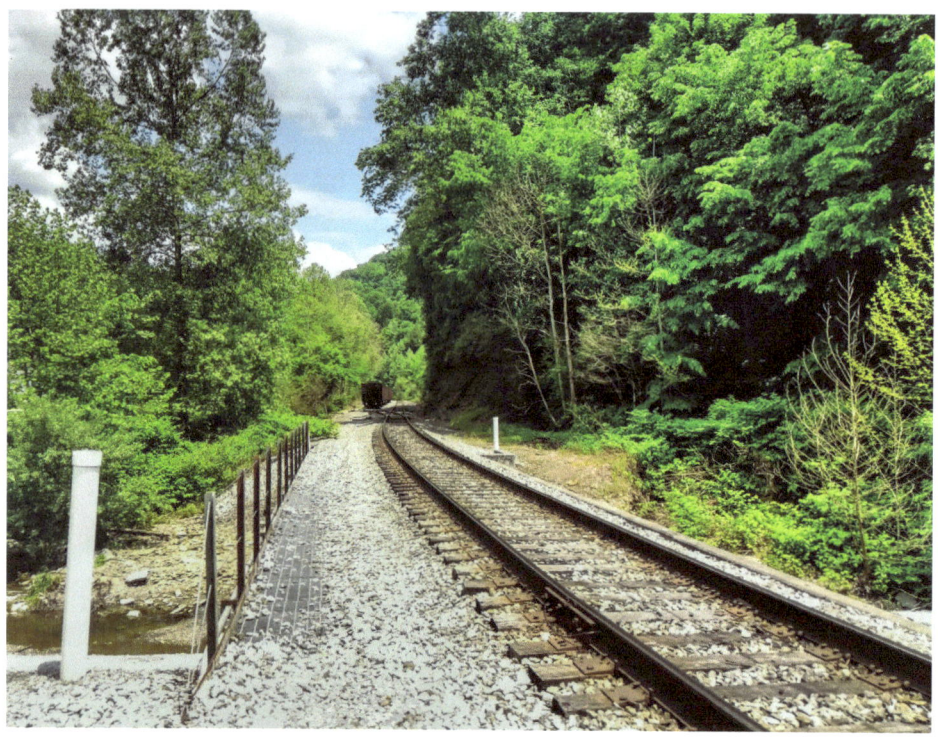

The first shipment of Coal to leave Harlan on a train occured in 1911.

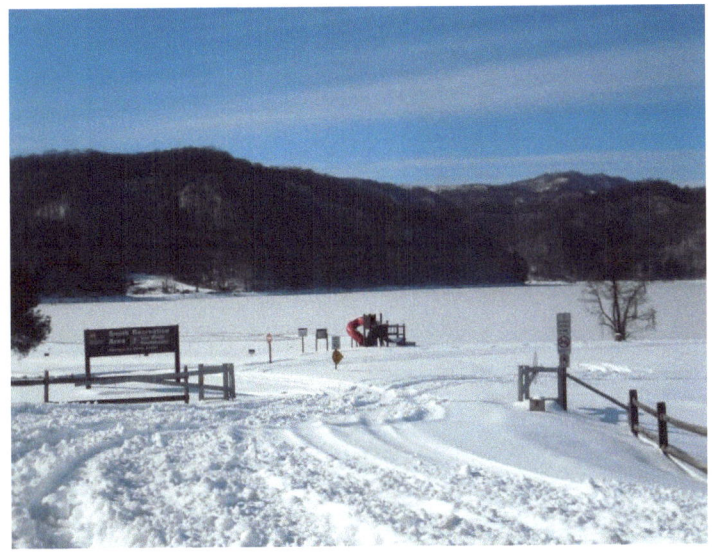

Martins Fork Lake Frozen Over During the Winter

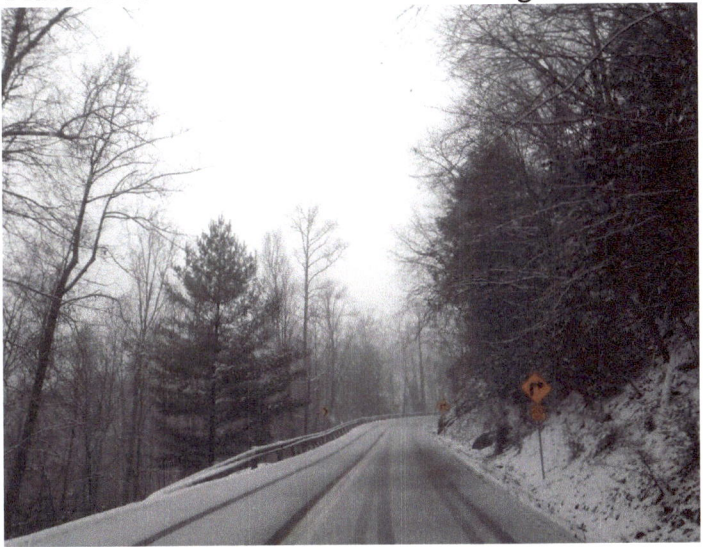

US 421 Crossing to Virginia

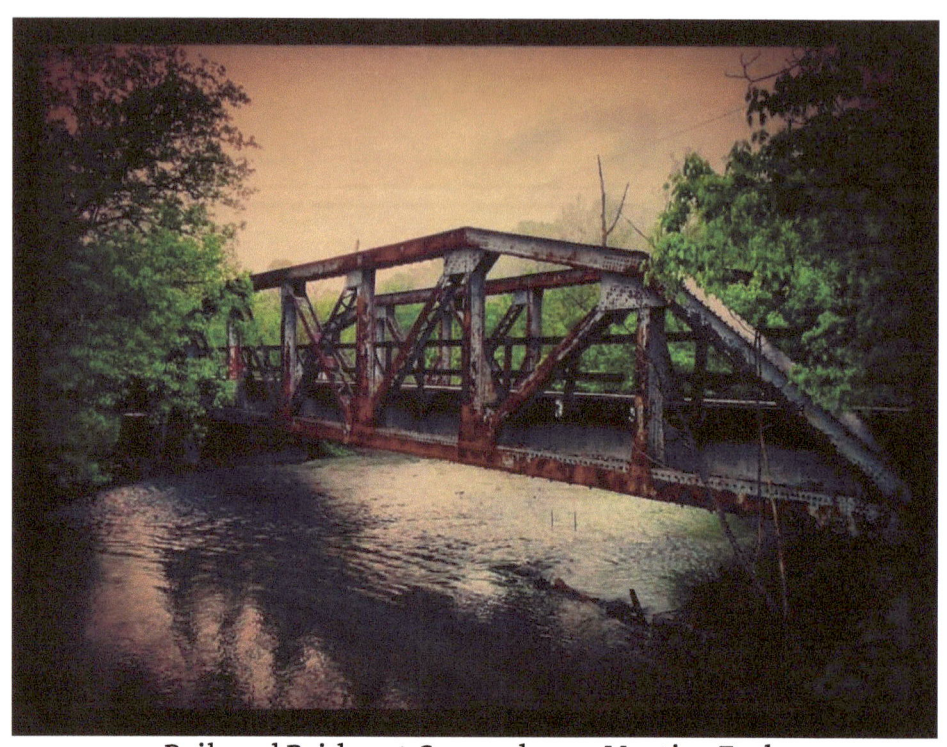

Railroad Bridge at Cawood over Martins Fork
(now demolished)

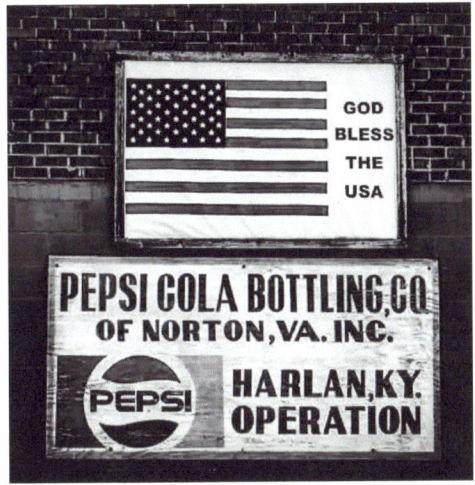

Loyall, Kentucky

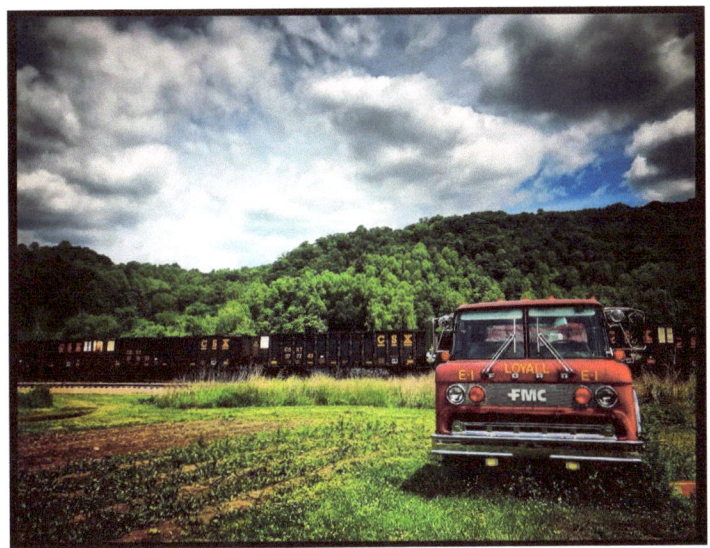

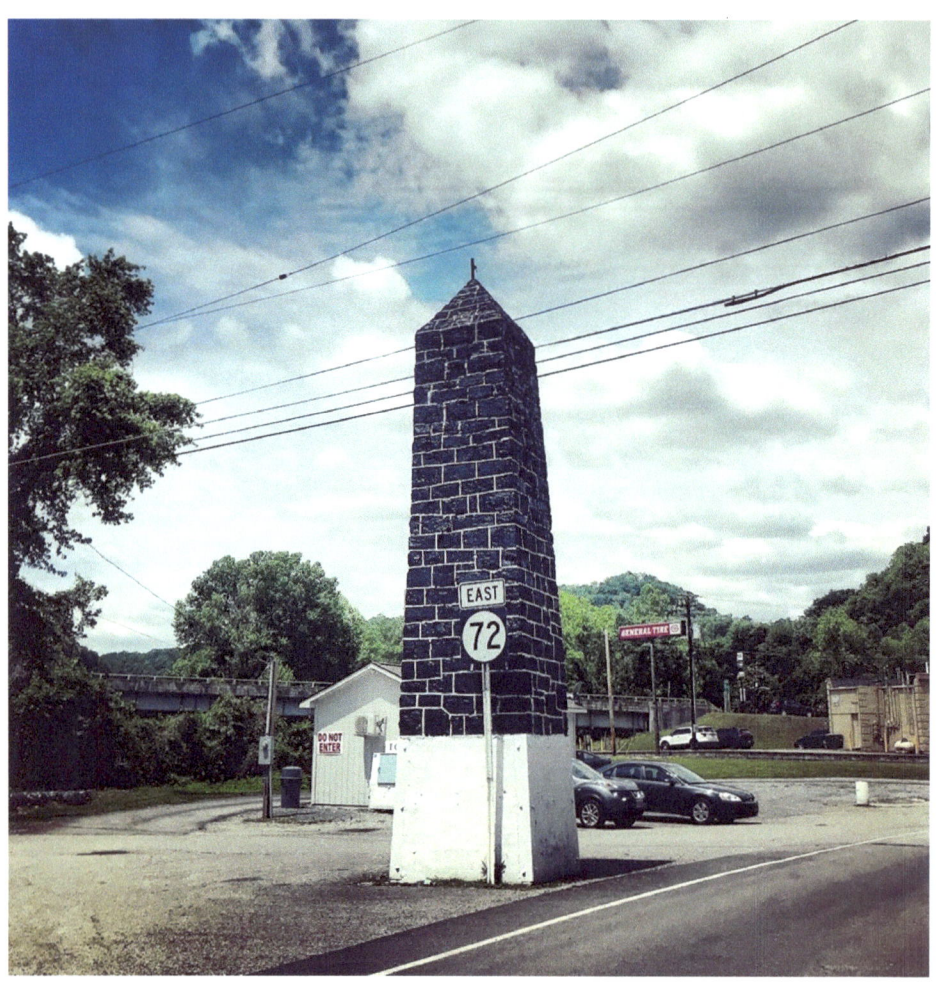

The Coal Monument at Baxter

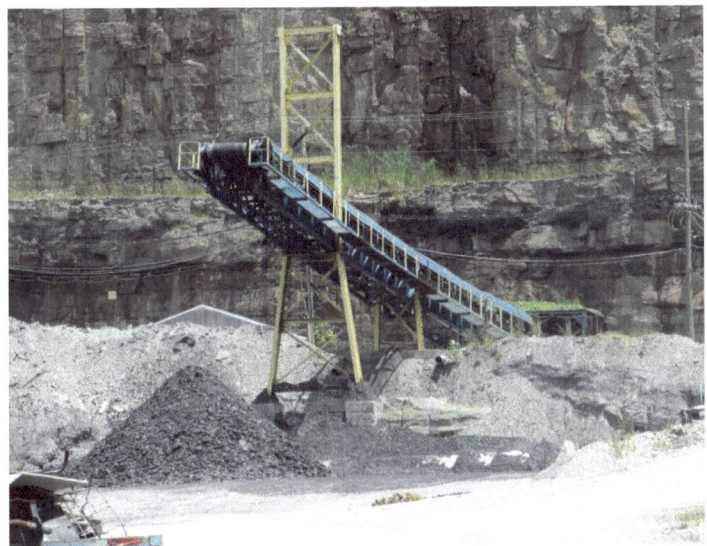

Harlan County Coal

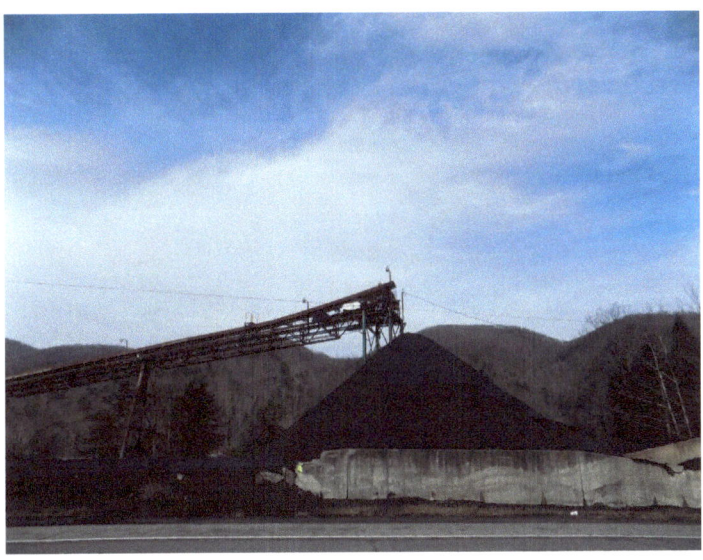

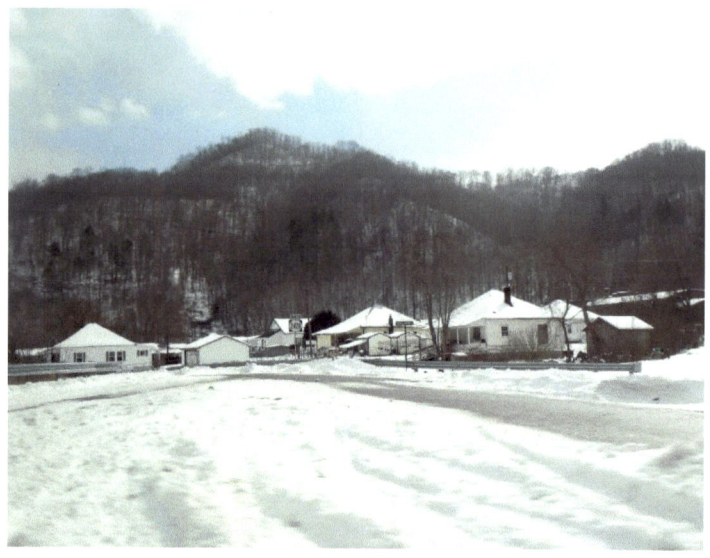

Grays Knob

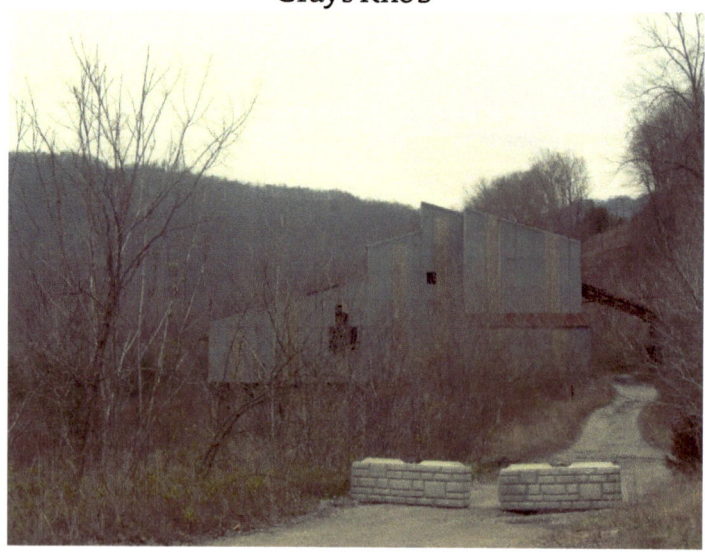

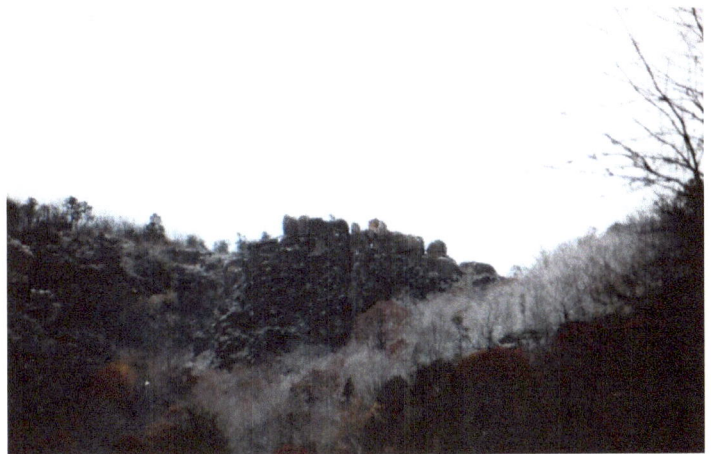
Locally known as the Chimney Rocks or the Castle Rocks

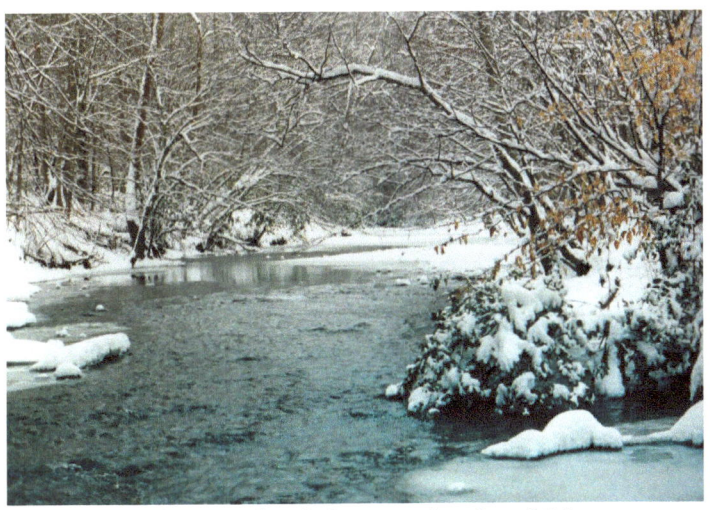
Martin's Fork of the Cumberland River

Main Street (KY 38) at Yocum Street (KY 215) in Evarts

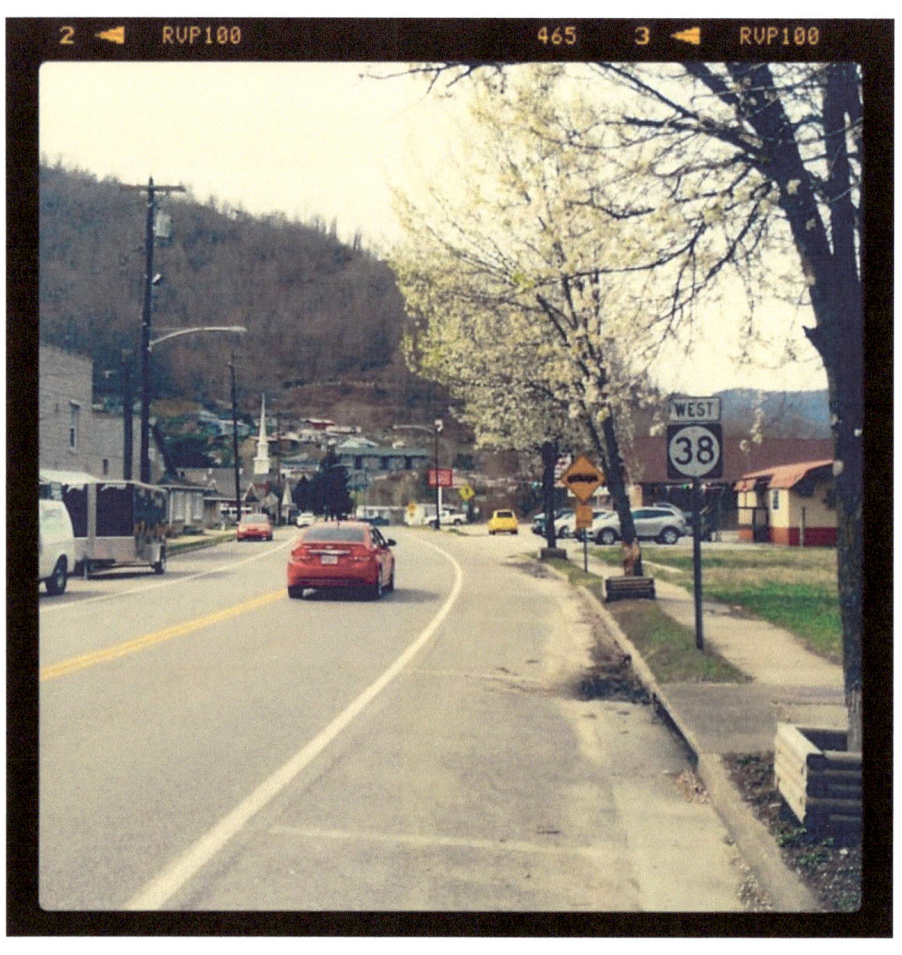

Closplint

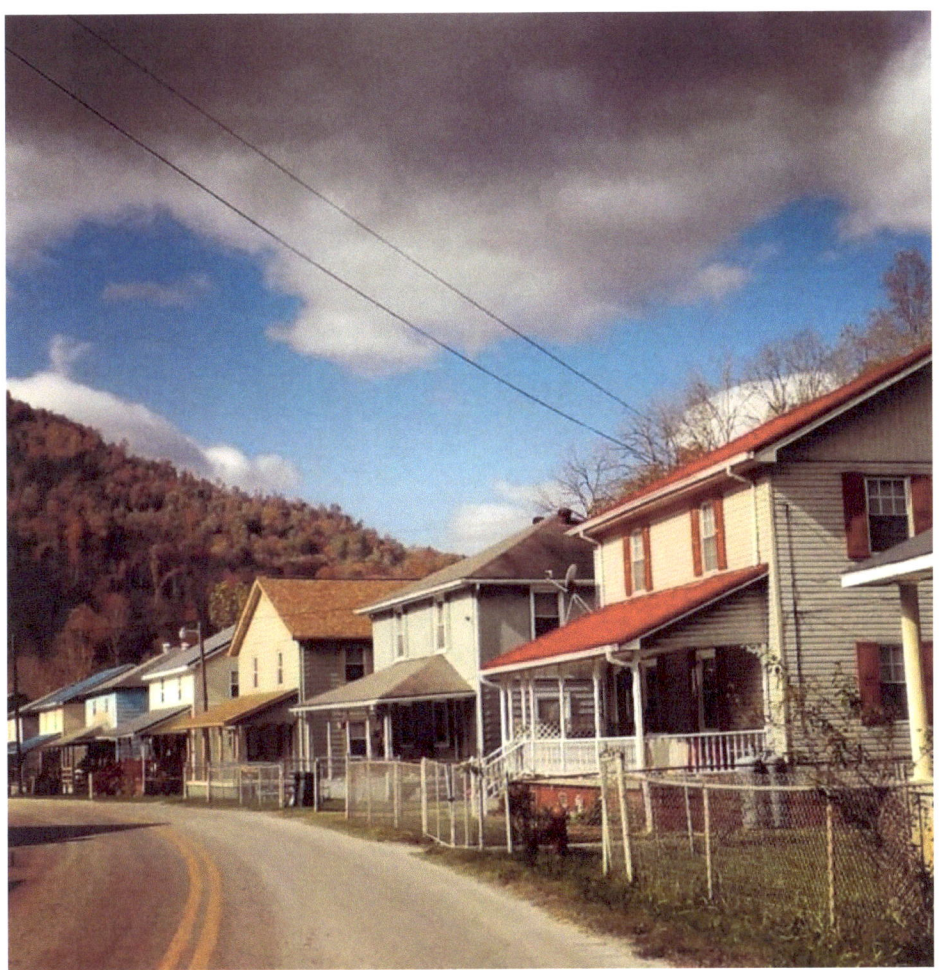

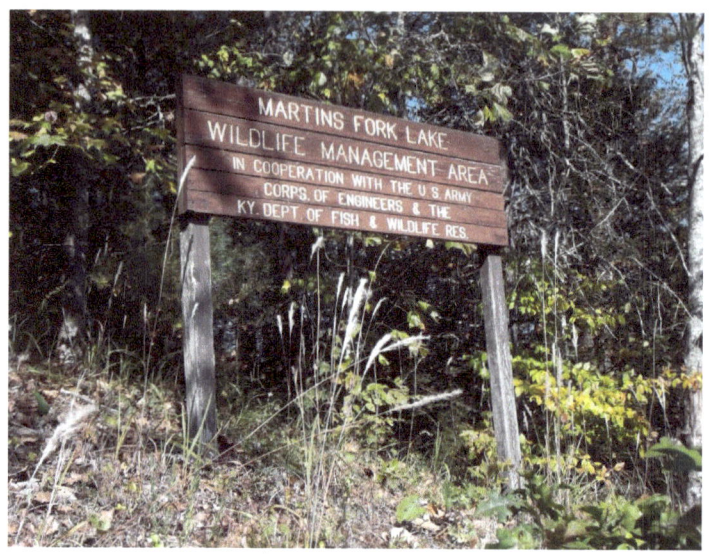

Martin's Fork Lake

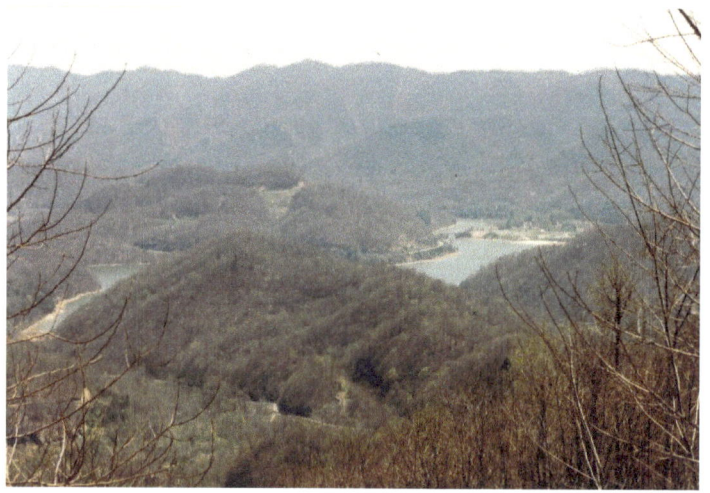

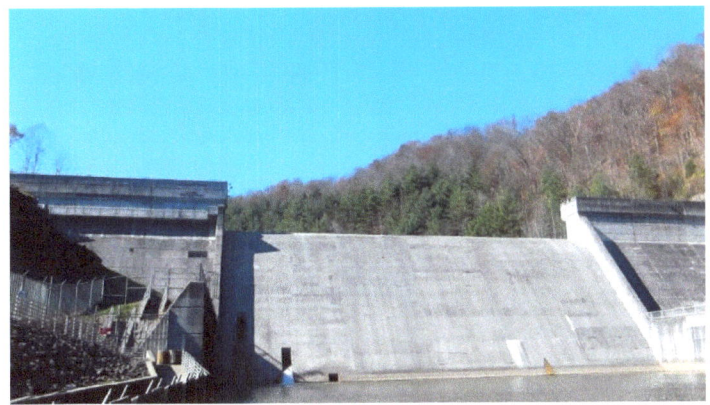

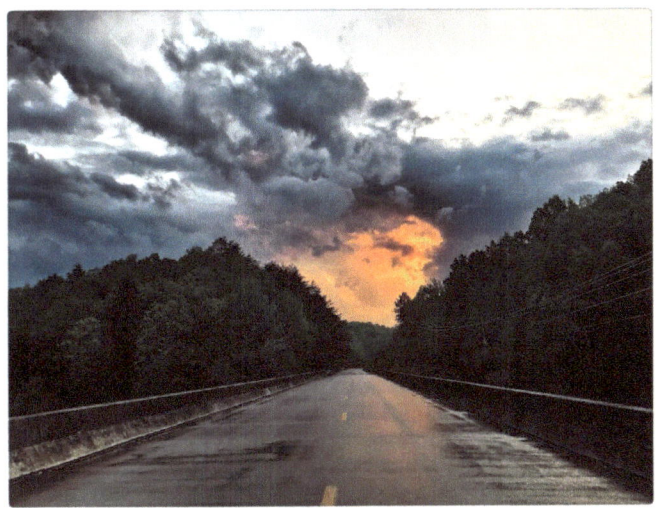

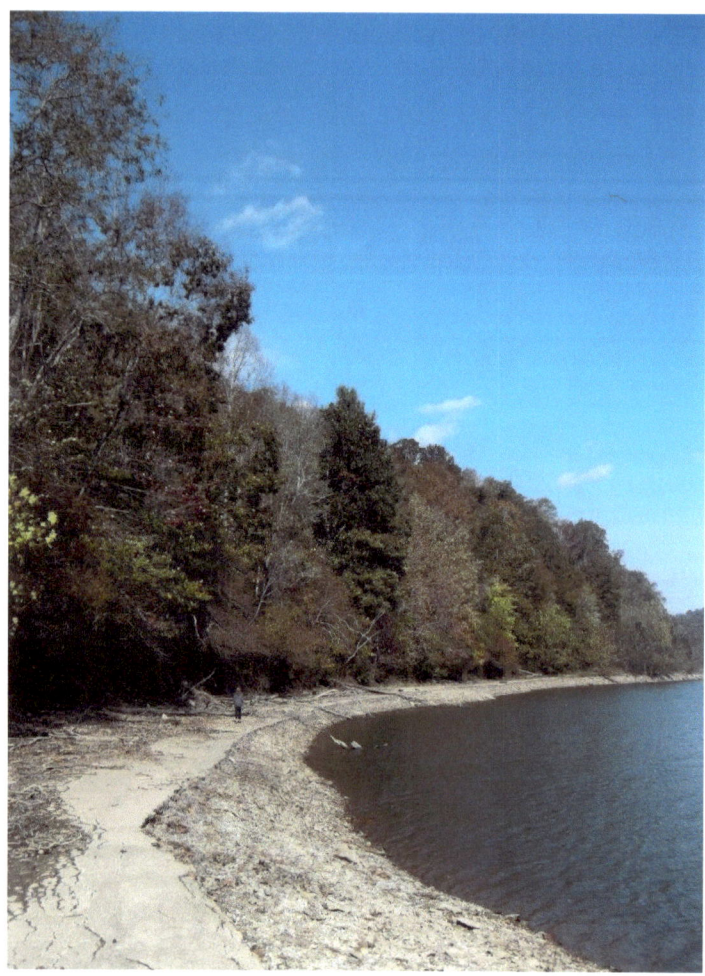

The old Route of KY 987 is still visable and walkable when the water is low at the lake. The road was reconstructed due east of the old route when the lake was built

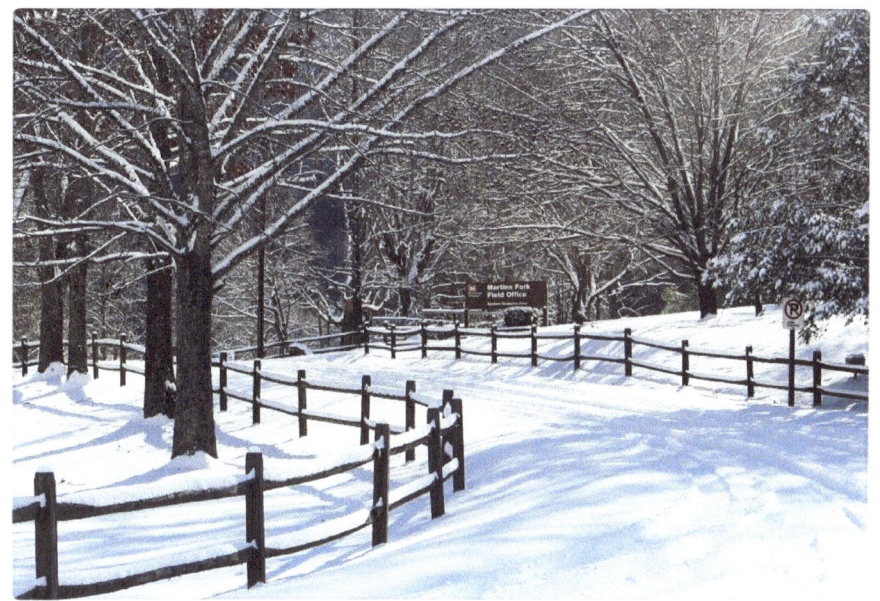

Martins Fork Lake

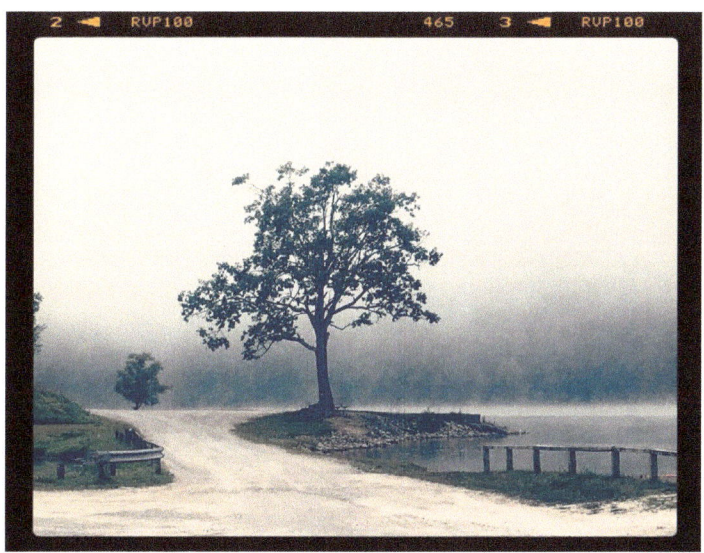

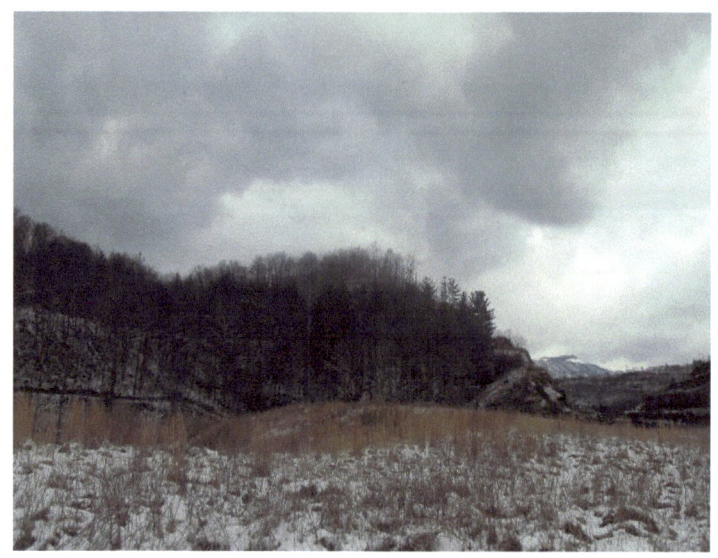

Old US 421 at Cranks Creek

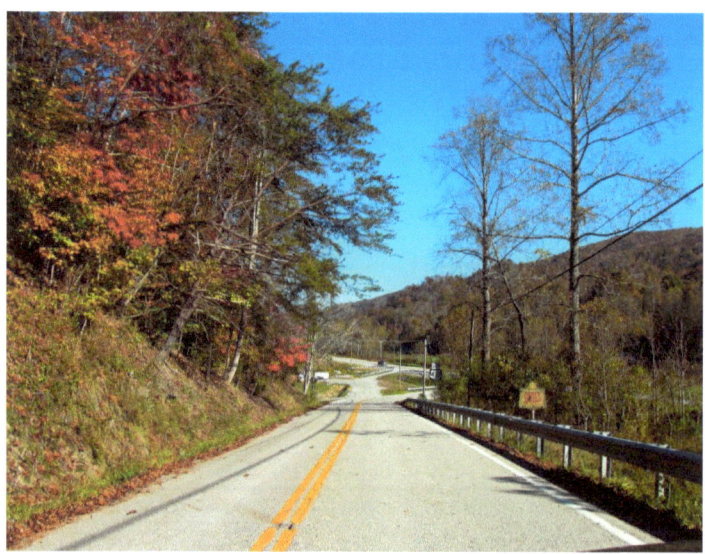

Highsplint Lake

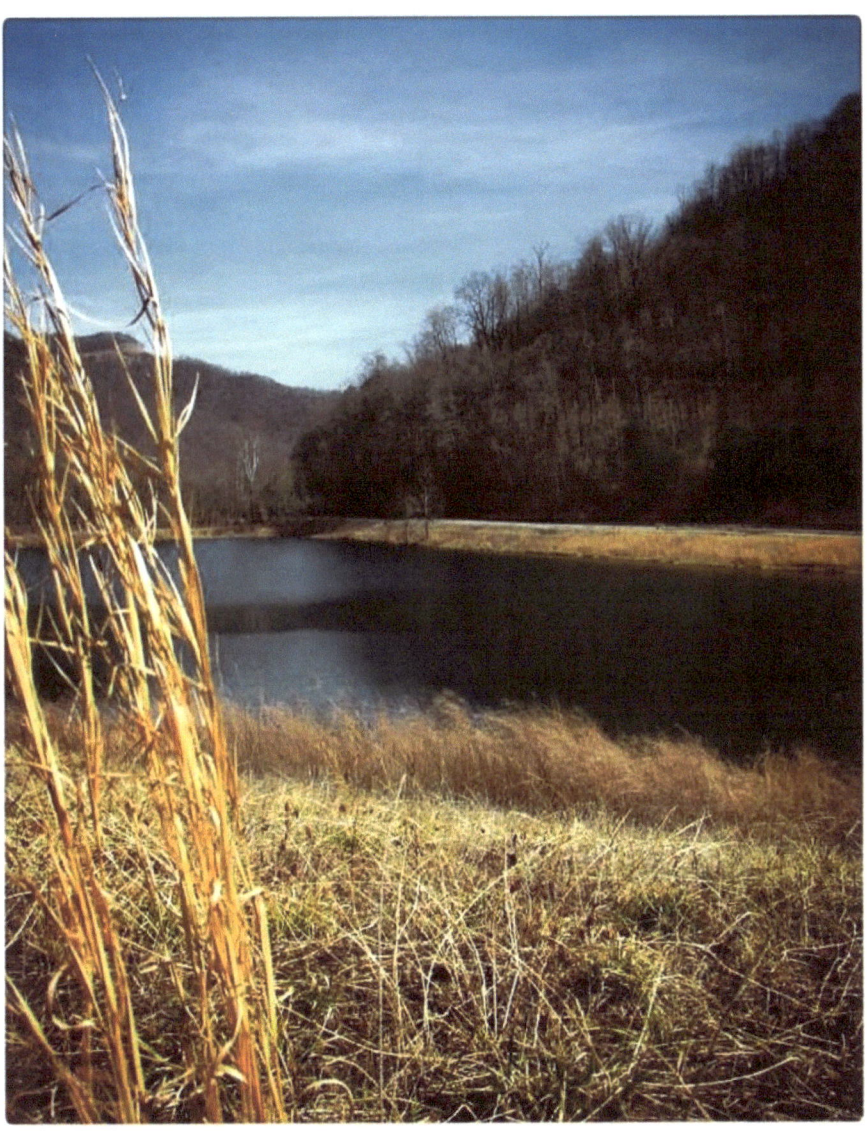

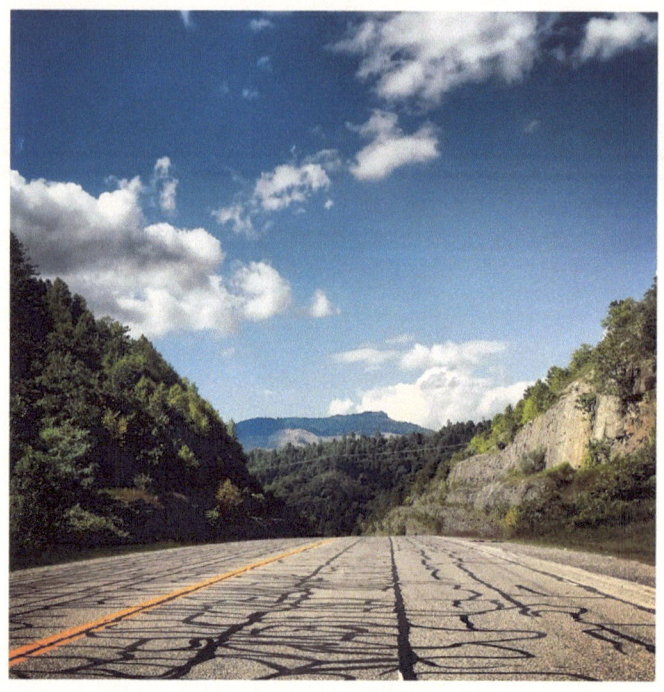

US 421 at the Crummies Cut Through South of Harlan.

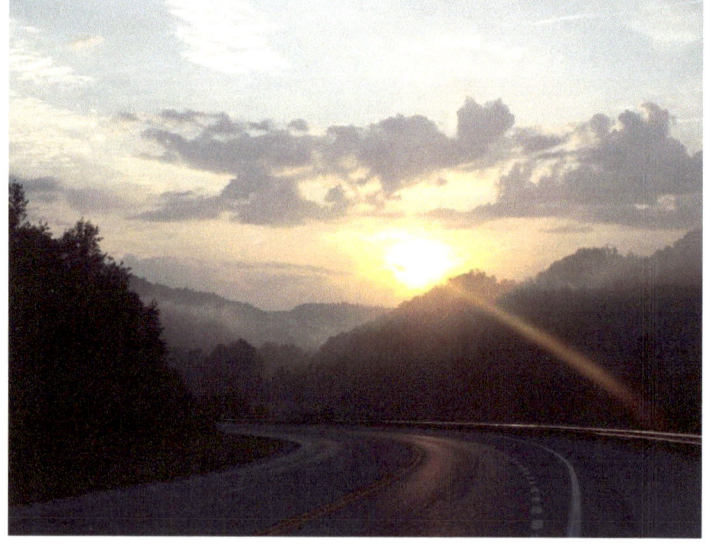

Middleton's Grocery at Smith

My family's store is pictured below. My mom and dad opperated this store all through my childhood. They closed it in 2000.

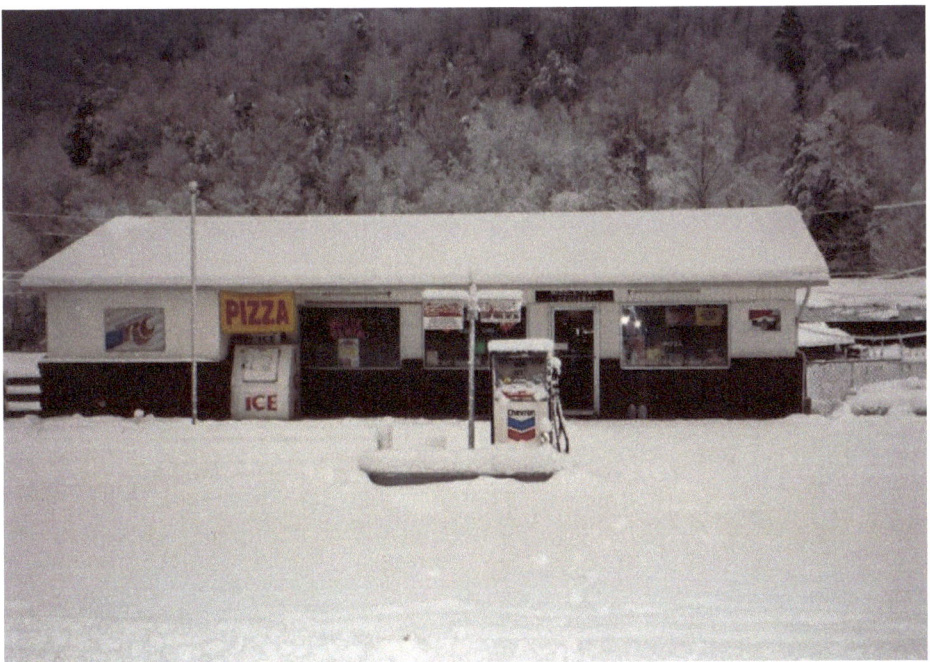

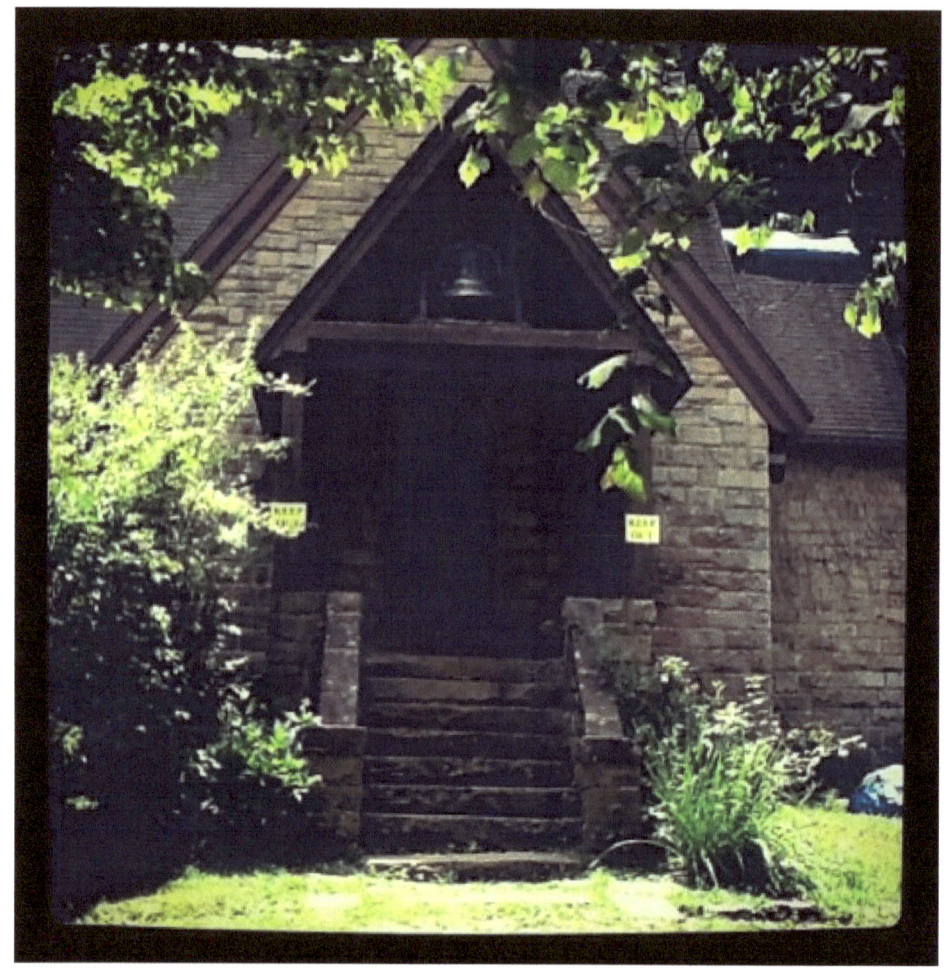

Pine Mountain Settlement School

Founded in 1913, the grounds are A National Historic Landmark, as a school and was started for children in the commonwealth's remote southeastern mountains and a social center for surrounding communities

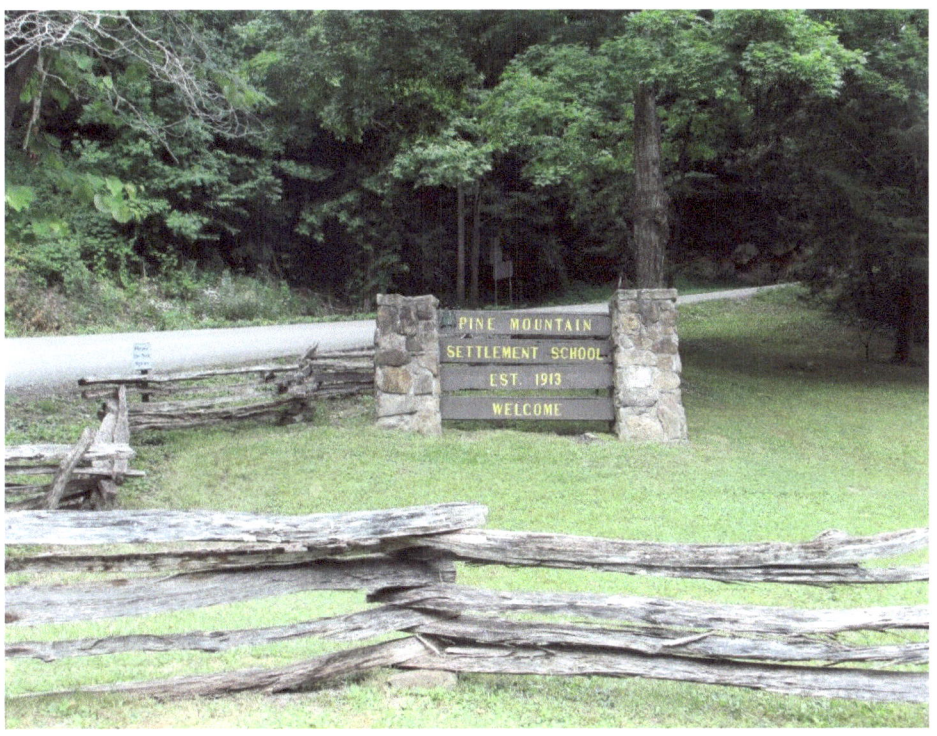

www.ingramcontent.com/pod-product-compliance
Lightning Source LLC
Chambersburg PA
CBHW040337220526
45473CB00009B/2715